The contents of this journal are

PERSONAL

and

CONFIDENTIAL.

DO NOT READ.

If found, please return to:

_____

Phone number:

_____

The Swimmer's Workout Log

by

Alex Haddox, M.Ed.

Published by

Palladium Education,® Inc.
6520 Platt Avenue, #174
West Hills, CA 91307-3218
PalladiumEducation.com

Copyright © 2016 by Palladium Education,® Inc.

Except as permitted under the Copyright Act of 1976, no part of this book may be reproduced by any electronic or mechanical means in any form including the use of information storage and retrieval systems, without permission in writing from the copyright owner.

Trademarks: "Palladium Education", and the Palladium Education, Inc. logo are trademarks of Palladium Education,® Inc.

ISBN-13:   978-1-939408-38-9

ISBN-10:   1-939408-38-5

To my swim coach John Apgar who planned thousands of training hours and stood above us on deck in blazing heat and freezing rain. Also to my parents who drove me to pre-dawn workouts, picked me up well after dark and sat for entire weekends on hard bleachers for a single 2-minute race.

The Swimmer's Workout Log

Table of Contents

How to Use This Log...iii

Sample Log Entry iv

Training Log... 1-95

Body Composition Log (skinfold).. 97

Body Measurements Log 97

Weight Log 99-100

How to Use This Log

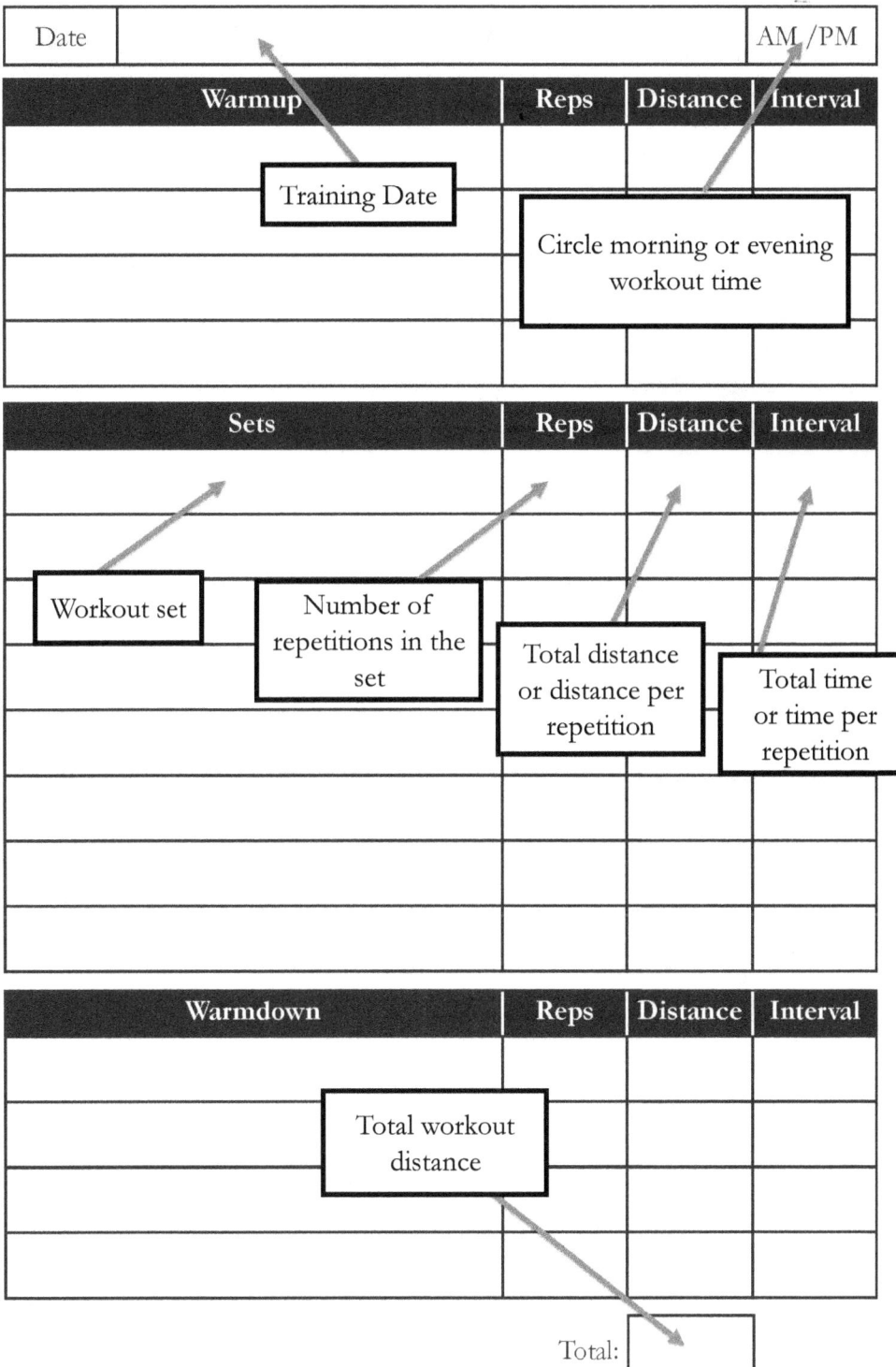

The Swimmer's Workout Log
Sample Log Entry

Date	7/14/2016			AM / PM
Warmup		**Reps**	**Distance**	**Interval**
FREESTYLE		3	100	1:45
KICK - IM		5	100	2:30

Sets	**Reps**	**Distance**	**Interval**
FREESTYLE	10	100	1:30
STRETCH	1	100	2:00
IM	5	100	1:50
STRETCH	1	100	2:00
KICK	8	100	2:40

Warmdown	**Reps**	**Distance**	**Interval**
FREESTYLE	3	200	4:00
PULL	3	200	4:00
KICK	3	200	4:00

Total: 5100

The Swimmer's Workout Log

Date		AM /PM

Warmup	Reps	Distance	Interval

Sets	Reps	Distance	Interval

Warmdown	Reps	Distance	Interval

Total:

The Swimmer's Workout Log

Date		AM /PM

Warmup	Reps	Distance	Interval

Sets	Reps	Distance	Interval

Warmdown	Reps	Distance	Interval

Total:

Palladium Education,® Inc.

The Swimmer's Workout Log

Date		AM /PM

Warmup	Reps	Distance	Interval

Sets	Reps	Distance	Interval

Warmdown	Reps	Distance	Interval

Total:

The Swimmer's Workout Log

Date		AM /PM

Warmup	Reps	Distance	Interval

Sets	Reps	Distance	Interval

Warmdown	Reps	Distance	Interval

Total:

Palladium Education,® Inc.

The Swimmer's Workout Log

Date		AM /PM

Warmup	Reps	Distance	Interval

Sets	Reps	Distance	Interval

Warmdown	Reps	Distance	Interval

Total:

PalladiumEducation.com

The Swimmer's Workout Log

Date		AM /PM

Warmup	Reps	Distance	Interval

Sets	Reps	Distance	Interval

Warmdown	Reps	Distance	Interval

Total:

Palladium Education,® Inc.

The Swimmer's Workout Log

Date		AM /PM

Warmup	Reps	Distance	Interval

Sets	Reps	Distance	Interval

Warmdown	Reps	Distance	Interval

Total:

The Swimmer's Workout Log

Date		AM /PM

Warmup	Reps	Distance	Interval

Sets	Reps	Distance	Interval

Warmdown	Reps	Distance	Interval

Total:

Palladium Education,® Inc.

The Swimmer's Workout Log

Date		AM /PM

Warmup	Reps	Distance	Interval

Sets	Reps	Distance	Interval

Warmdown	Reps	Distance	Interval

Total:

The Swimmer's Workout Log

Date				AM /PM

Warmup	Reps	Distance	Interval

Sets	Reps	Distance	Interval

Warmdown	Reps	Distance	Interval

Total:

The Swimmer's Workout Log

Date		AM /PM

Warmup	Reps	Distance	Interval

Sets	Reps	Distance	Interval

Warmdown	Reps	Distance	Interval

Total:

PalladiumEducation.com

The Swimmer's Workout Log

Date		AM /PM

Warmup	Reps	Distance	Interval

Sets	Reps	Distance	Interval

Warmdown	Reps	Distance	Interval

Total:

Palladium Education,® Inc.

The Swimmer's Workout Log

Date		AM /PM

Warmup	**Reps**	**Distance**	**Interval**

Sets	**Reps**	**Distance**	**Interval**

Warmdown	**Reps**	**Distance**	**Interval**

Total:

The Swimmer's Workout Log

Date		AM /PM

Warmup	Reps	Distance	Interval

Sets	Reps	Distance	Interval

Warmdown	Reps	Distance	Interval

Total:

The Swimmer's Workout Log

Date		AM /PM

Warmup	Reps	Distance	Interval

Sets	Reps	Distance	Interval

Warmdown	Reps	Distance	Interval

Total:

The Swimmer's Workout Log

Date		AM /PM

Warmup	Reps	Distance	Interval

Sets	Reps	Distance	Interval

Warmdown	Reps	Distance	Interval

Total:

The Swimmer's Workout Log

Date		AM /PM

Warmup	Reps	Distance	Interval

Sets	Reps	Distance	Interval

Warmdown	Reps	Distance	Interval

Total:

The Swimmer's Workout Log

Date		AM /PM

Warmup	Reps	Distance	Interval

Sets	Reps	Distance	Interval

Warmdown	Reps	Distance	Interval

Total:

The Swimmer's Workout Log

Date		AM /PM

Warmup	Reps	Distance	Interval

Sets	Reps	Distance	Interval

Warmdown	Reps	Distance	Interval

Total:

The Swimmer's Workout Log

Date		AM /PM

Warmup	Reps	Distance	Interval

Sets	Reps	Distance	Interval

Warmdown	Reps	Distance	Interval

Total:

The Swimmer's Workout Log

Date		AM /PM

Warmup	Reps	Distance	Interval

Sets	Reps	Distance	Interval

Warmdown	Reps	Distance	Interval

Total:

The Swimmer's Workout Log

Date		AM /PM

Warmup	Reps	Distance	Interval

Sets	Reps	Distance	Interval

Warmdown	Reps	Distance	Interval

Total:

The Swimmer's Workout Log

Date		AM /PM

Warmup	Reps	Distance	Interval

Sets	Reps	Distance	Interval

Warmdown	Reps	Distance	Interval

Total:

The Swimmer's Workout Log

Date		AM /PM

Warmup	Reps	Distance	Interval

Sets	Reps	Distance	Interval

Warmdown	Reps	Distance	Interval

Total:

The Swimmer's Workout Log

Date		AM /PM

Warmup	Reps	Distance	Interval

Sets	Reps	Distance	Interval

Warmdown	Reps	Distance	Interval

Total:

The Swimmer's Workout Log

Date		AM /PM

Warmup	Reps	Distance	Interval

Sets	Reps	Distance	Interval

Warmdown	Reps	Distance	Interval

Total:

The Swimmer's Workout Log

Date		AM /PM

Warmup	Reps	Distance	Interval

Sets	Reps	Distance	Interval

Warmdown	Reps	Distance	Interval

Total:

The Swimmer's Workout Log

Date		AM /PM

Warmup	Reps	Distance	Interval

Sets	Reps	Distance	Interval

Warmdown	Reps	Distance	Interval

Total:

Palladium Education,® Inc.

The Swimmer's Workout Log

Date		AM /PM

Warmup	Reps	Distance	Interval

Sets	Reps	Distance	Interval

Warmdown	Reps	Distance	Interval

Total:

The Swimmer's Workout Log

Date		AM /PM

Warmup	Reps	Distance	Interval

Sets	Reps	Distance	Interval

Warmdown	Reps	Distance	Interval

Total:

Palladium Education,® Inc.

The Swimmer's Workout Log

Date		AM /PM

Warmup	Reps	Distance	Interval

Sets	Reps	Distance	Interval

Warmdown	Reps	Distance	Interval

Total:

The Swimmer's Workout Log

Date		AM /PM

Warmup	Reps	Distance	Interval

Sets	Reps	Distance	Interval

Warmdown	Reps	Distance	Interval

Total:

The Swimmer's Workout Log

Date		AM /PM

Warmup	Reps	Distance	Interval

Sets	Reps	Distance	Interval

Warmdown	Reps	Distance	Interval

Total:

The Swimmer's Workout Log

Date		AM /PM

Warmup	Reps	Distance	Interval

Sets	Reps	Distance	Interval

Warmdown	Reps	Distance	Interval

Total:

The Swimmer's Workout Log

Date		AM /PM

Warmup	Reps	Distance	Interval

Sets	Reps	Distance	Interval

Warmdown	Reps	Distance	Interval

Total:

The Swimmer's Workout Log

Date		AM /PM

Warmup	Reps	Distance	Interval

Sets	Reps	Distance	Interval

Warmdown	Reps	Distance	Interval

Total:

The Swimmer's Workout Log

Date		AM /PM

Warmup	Reps	Distance	Interval

Sets	Reps	Distance	Interval

Warmdown	Reps	Distance	Interval

Total:

The Swimmer's Workout Log

Date		AM /PM

Warmup	Reps	Distance	Interval

Sets	Reps	Distance	Interval

Warmdown	Reps	Distance	Interval

Total:

The Swimmer's Workout Log

Date		AM /PM

Warmup	Reps	Distance	Interval

Sets	Reps	Distance	Interval

Warmdown	Reps	Distance	Interval

Total:

The Swimmer's Workout Log

Date				AM /PM

Warmup	Reps	Distance	Interval

Sets	Reps	Distance	Interval

Warmdown	Reps	Distance	Interval

Total:

The Swimmer's Workout Log

Date		AM /PM

Warmup	Reps	Distance	Interval

Sets	Reps	Distance	Interval

Warmdown	Reps	Distance	Interval

Total:

The Swimmer's Workout Log

Date		AM /PM

Warmup	Reps	Distance	Interval

Sets	Reps	Distance	Interval

Warmdown	Reps	Distance	Interval

Total:

Palladium Education,® Inc.

The Swimmer's Workout Log

Date		AM /PM

Warmup	Reps	Distance	Interval

Sets	Reps	Distance	Interval

Warmdown	Reps	Distance	Interval

Total:

The Swimmer's Workout Log

Date		AM /PM

Warmup	Reps	Distance	Interval

Sets	Reps	Distance	Interval

Warmdown	Reps	Distance	Interval

Total:

The Swimmer's Workout Log

Date		AM /PM

Warmup	Reps	Distance	Interval

Sets	Reps	Distance	Interval

Warmdown	Reps	Distance	Interval

Total:

PalladiumEducation.com

The Swimmer's Workout Log

Date		AM /PM

Warmup	Reps	Distance	Interval

Sets	Reps	Distance	Interval

Warmdown	Reps	Distance	Interval

Total:

The Swimmer's Workout Log

Date		AM /PM

Warmup	Reps	Distance	Interval

Sets	Reps	Distance	Interval

Warmdown	Reps	Distance	Interval

Total:

The Swimmer's Workout Log

Date		AM /PM

Warmup	Reps	Distance	Interval

Sets	Reps	Distance	Interval

Warmdown	Reps	Distance	Interval

Total:

Palladium Education,® Inc.

The Swimmer's Workout Log

Date		AM /PM

Warmup	Reps	Distance	Interval

Sets	Reps	Distance	Interval

Warmdown	Reps	Distance	Interval

Total:

The Swimmer's Workout Log

Date		AM /PM

Warmup	Reps	Distance	Interval

Sets	Reps	Distance	Interval

Warmdown	Reps	Distance	Interval

Total:

The Swimmer's Workout Log

Date		AM /PM

Warmup	Reps	Distance	Interval

Sets	Reps	Distance	Interval

Warmdown	Reps	Distance	Interval

Total:

PalladiumEducation.com

The Swimmer's Workout Log

Date		AM /PM

Warmup	Reps	Distance	Interval

Sets	Reps	Distance	Interval

Warmdown	Reps	Distance	Interval

Total:

The Swimmer's Workout Log

Date		AM /PM

Warmup	Reps	Distance	Interval

Sets	Reps	Distance	Interval

Warmdown	Reps	Distance	Interval

Total:

PalladiumEducation.com

The Swimmer's Workout Log

Date		AM /PM

Warmup	Reps	Distance	Interval

Sets	Reps	Distance	Interval

Warmdown	Reps	Distance	Interval

Total:

The Swimmer's Workout Log

Date		AM /PM

Warmup	Reps	Distance	Interval

Sets	Reps	Distance	Interval

Warmdown	Reps	Distance	Interval

Total:

The Swimmer's Workout Log

Date		AM /PM

Warmup	Reps	Distance	Interval

Sets	Reps	Distance	Interval

Warmdown	Reps	Distance	Interval

Total:

Palladium Education,® Inc.

The Swimmer's Workout Log

Date		AM /PM

Warmup	Reps	Distance	Interval

Sets	Reps	Distance	Interval

Warmdown	Reps	Distance	Interval

Total:

The Swimmer's Workout Log

Date		AM /PM

Warmup	Reps	Distance	Interval

Sets	Reps	Distance	Interval

Warmdown	Reps	Distance	Interval

Total:

The Swimmer's Workout Log

Date		AM /PM

Warmup	Reps	Distance	Interval

Sets	Reps	Distance	Interval

Warmdown	Reps	Distance	Interval

Total:

The Swimmer's Workout Log

Date		AM /PM

Warmup	Reps	Distance	Interval

Sets	Reps	Distance	Interval

Warmdown	Reps	Distance	Interval

Total:

The Swimmer's Workout Log

Date		AM /PM

Warmup	Reps	Distance	Interval

Sets	Reps	Distance	Interval

Warmdown	Reps	Distance	Interval

Total:

The Swimmer's Workout Log

Date		AM /PM

Warmup	Reps	Distance	Interval

Sets	Reps	Distance	Interval

Warmdown	Reps	Distance	Interval

Total:

Palladium Education,® Inc.

The Swimmer's Workout Log

Date		AM /PM

Warmup	Reps	Distance	Interval

Sets	Reps	Distance	Interval

Warmdown	Reps	Distance	Interval

Total:

The Swimmer's Workout Log

Date		AM /PM

Warmup	Reps	Distance	Interval

Sets	Reps	Distance	Interval

Warmdown	Reps	Distance	Interval

Total:

Palladium Education,® Inc.

The Swimmer's Workout Log

Date		AM /PM

Warmup	Reps	Distance	Interval

Sets	Reps	Distance	Interval

Warmdown	Reps	Distance	Interval

Total:

The Swimmer's Workout Log

Date		AM /PM

Warmup	Reps	Distance	Interval

Sets	Reps	Distance	Interval

Warmdown	Reps	Distance	Interval

Total:

The Swimmer's Workout Log

Date		AM /PM

Warmup	Reps	Distance	Interval

Sets	Reps	Distance	Interval

Warmdown	Reps	Distance	Interval

Total:

The Swimmer's Workout Log

Date		AM /PM

Warmup	Reps	Distance	Interval

Sets	Reps	Distance	Interval

Warmdown	Reps	Distance	Interval

Total:

Palladium Education,® Inc.

The Swimmer's Workout Log

Date		AM /PM

Warmup	Reps	Distance	Interval

Sets	Reps	Distance	Interval

Warmdown	Reps	Distance	Interval

Total:

The Swimmer's Workout Log

Date		AM /PM

Warmup	Reps	Distance	Interval

Sets	Reps	Distance	Interval

Warmdown	Reps	Distance	Interval

Total:

The Swimmer's Workout Log

Date		AM /PM

Warmup	Reps	Distance	Interval

Sets	Reps	Distance	Interval

Warmdown	Reps	Distance	Interval

Total:

PalladiumEducation.com

The Swimmer's Workout Log

Date		AM /PM

Warmup	Reps	Distance	Interval

Sets	Reps	Distance	Interval

Warmdown	Reps	Distance	Interval

Total:

Palladium Education,® Inc.

The Swimmer's Workout Log

Date		AM /PM

Warmup	Reps	Distance	Interval

Sets	Reps	Distance	Interval

Warmdown	Reps	Distance	Interval

Total:

The Swimmer's Workout Log

Date		AM /PM

Warmup	Reps	Distance	Interval

Sets	Reps	Distance	Interval

Warmdown	Reps	Distance	Interval

Total:

The Swimmer's Workout Log

Date		AM /PM

Warmup	Reps	Distance	Interval

Sets	Reps	Distance	Interval

Warmdown	Reps	Distance	Interval

Total:

The Swimmer's Workout Log

Date		AM /PM

Warmup	Reps	Distance	Interval

Sets	Reps	Distance	Interval

Warmdown	Reps	Distance	Interval

Total:

The Swimmer's Workout Log

Date		AM /PM

Warmup	Reps	Distance	Interval

Sets	Reps	Distance	Interval

Warmdown	Reps	Distance	Interval

Total:

PalladiumEducation.com

The Swimmer's Workout Log

Date		AM /PM

Warmup	Reps	Distance	Interval

Sets	Reps	Distance	Interval

Warmdown	Reps	Distance	Interval

Total:

The Swimmer's Workout Log

Date		AM /PM

Warmup	Reps	Distance	Interval

Sets	Reps	Distance	Interval

Warmdown	Reps	Distance	Interval

Total:

The Swimmer's Workout Log

Date		AM /PM

Warmup	Reps	Distance	Interval

Sets	Reps	Distance	Interval

Warmdown	Reps	Distance	Interval

Total:

The Swimmer's Workout Log

Date		AM /PM

Warmup	Reps	Distance	Interval

Sets	Reps	Distance	Interval

Warmdown	Reps	Distance	Interval

Total:

PalladiumEducation.com

The Swimmer's Workout Log

Date		AM /PM

Warmup	Reps	Distance	Interval

Sets	Reps	Distance	Interval

Warmdown	Reps	Distance	Interval

Total:

Palladium Education,® Inc.

The Swimmer's Workout Log

Date		AM /PM

Warmup	Reps	Distance	Interval

Sets	Reps	Distance	Interval

Warmdown	Reps	Distance	Interval

Total:

PalladiumEducation.com

The Swimmer's Workout Log

Date		AM /PM

Warmup	Reps	Distance	Interval

Sets	Reps	Distance	Interval

Warmdown	Reps	Distance	Interval

Total:

The Swimmer's Workout Log

Date		AM /PM

Warmup	Reps	Distance	Interval

Sets	Reps	Distance	Interval

Warmdown	Reps	Distance	Interval

Total:

PalladiumEducation.com

The Swimmer's Workout Log

Date		AM /PM

Warmup	Reps	Distance	Interval

Sets	Reps	Distance	Interval

Warmdown	Reps	Distance	Interval

Total:

The Swimmer's Workout Log

Date		AM /PM

Warmup	Reps	Distance	Interval

Sets	Reps	Distance	Interval

Warmdown	Reps	Distance	Interval

Total:

The Swimmer's Workout Log

Date		AM /PM

Warmup	Reps	Distance	Interval

Sets	Reps	Distance	Interval

Warmdown	Reps	Distance	Interval

Total:

The Swimmer's Workout Log

Date		AM /PM

Warmup	Reps	Distance	Interval

Sets	Reps	Distance	Interval

Warmdown	Reps	Distance	Interval

Total:

The Swimmer's Workout Log

Date		AM /PM

Warmup	Reps	Distance	Interval

Sets	Reps	Distance	Interval

Warmdown	Reps	Distance	Interval

Total:

The Swimmer's Workout Log

Date		AM /PM

Warmup	Reps	Distance	Interval

Sets	Reps	Distance	Interval

Warmdown	Reps	Distance	Interval

Total:

The Swimmer's Workout Log

Date		AM /PM

Warmup	Reps	Distance	Interval

Sets	Reps	Distance	Interval

Warmdown	Reps	Distance	Interval

Total:

The Swimmer's Workout Log

Date		AM /PM

Warmup	Reps	Distance	Interval

Sets	Reps	Distance	Interval

Warmdown	Reps	Distance	Interval

Total:

The Swimmer's Workout Log

Date		AM /PM

Warmup	Reps	Distance	Interval

Sets	Reps	Distance	Interval

Warmdown	Reps	Distance	Interval

Total:

The Swimmer's Workout Log

Date		AM /PM

Warmup	Reps	Distance	Interval

Sets	Reps	Distance	Interval

Warmdown	Reps	Distance	Interval

Total:

The Swimmer's Workout Log

Body Composition Log (skinfold) Measurements are in milimeters (mm)

Date	%	Triceps	Thigh	Suprailiac	Pectoral	Subscapula	Midaxilla	Abdomen

Body Measurements Log

Date	Neck	Chest	L. Arm	Abdomen	Hips	L. Thigh	L. Calf

The Swimmer's Workout Log

Weight Log

Date	Weight	Date	Weight

Weight Log

Date	Weight	Date	Weight

www.ingramcontent.com/pod-product-compliance
Lightning Source LLC
Chambersburg PA
CBHW071303040426
42444CB00009B/1844